GRAMMAR
CORRECTION
EXERCISES

ESL English Grammar Correction

BY MIRIAM MURPHY

MW00885840

Copyright © Miriam Murphy 2018

All rights reserved. No part of this publication may be reproduced, distributed, or transmitted in any form or by any means, including photocopying, recording or any other electronic methods, without prior written consent from the author.

GRAMMAR CORRECTION EXERCISES

Error correction in the ESL classroom is one of the stepping stones to accuracy in English. Recognizing errors shows that a student is making progress in his or her studies.

This publication has been put together with authentic writings from low level ESL students up to an Intermediate level.

Can you recognize some of the most common errors made by second language English learners? Test yourself and find out, then go to the answers to check if you were right or wrong.

Notes are given after each correction as to why it is an error. If you can identify all 165 errors then great! It means you've come a long way.

Now let's get started shall we?

Exercise one

There are nine errors in the following passage. Find them and correct them then check your answers at the end of the passage.

I live at a small town near London. I live with my mother, father, brother and sister.

My names John and my sisters name's Jill.

I have fourteen years old and my sister has sixteen years.

My mother's names Mary and my fathers names Tom.

We also have a dog who's name's Rover. He is lively dog. He loves go on long walks.

Check your answers

Error one: I live **at** a small town near London

Error: the use of the wrong preposition –**at**- a small town near London.

Correction: I live **in** a small town near London.

Error two: My nam**es** John.

Error: '**names**' = the plural of '**name**'. We need to use the verb '**be**'–is-contracted to '**s**)

Correction: My name**'s** John.

Error three: My sister**s** name's Jill.

Error: '**sisters**' = the plural of '**sister**'. We need to use the genitive case '**s**)

Correction: My sister**'s** name's Jill = the name of my sister

1

Error four: I *have* fourteen years old.

Error: the use the verb '**have**' to say how old a person is when in English we need a form of the verb '**be**'.

Correction: I **am** fourteen years old, contracted to 'I**'m** fourteen years old'.

Error five: My sister *has* sixteen year*s*.

Error: double error. The first error is the same as the previous one-*error four*. We use the verb '**be**' for age. '**Sixteen years**' is an error. We can say either **sixteen** or **sixteen years old** but *never* **sixteen years**).

Correction: My sister **is** sixteen **years old** or my sister**'s sixteen** (verb '**be**' contracted in third person singular)

Error six: My mother's name*s* Mary and my father*s* name*s* Tom.

Error: triple error. '**Names**' = the plural of name. We need the possessive form with an apostrophe before the '**s**. The same applies to '**fathers**' which is the plural of '**father**'. We need to add an apostrophe to make the noun '**father**' become the possessive (the genitive case) and we need to add an apostrophe before the '**s**' in '**names**' to indicate the presence of the verb '**be**' and not the plural of name – names.

Correction: My mother's name**'s** Mary and my father**'s** name**'s** Tom = the name of my mother is Mary and the name of my father is Tom.

Error seven: We also have a dog who*'s* name's Rover.

Error: **who's** = **who is**. We need to use '**whose**' which is pronounced identically to '**who's**'. We use '**whose**' to indicate that the object of the sentence belongs to (is possessed by) the subject of the sentence. '**Dog**' is the subject and '**name**' is the object.

Correction: We also have a dog **whose** name's Rover = We also have a dog. His name's Rover. Link the two sentences to make one by removing the possessive adjective '**his**' and replacing it with '**whose**'.

<u>Error eight</u>: He is lively dog.

<u>Error</u>: omission of the indefinite article '**a**'.

<u>Correction</u>: He is a lively dog. (Contracted = he's a lively dog). For animals we normally use the subject pronoun '**it**', if we do not know the sex of the animal. If we know the sex, or the animal is a family pet, we can replace '**it**' with 'he or she'.

<u>Notes</u>: This is extremely common among Indian speakers of English. '**A**' indicates '**one of a kind**'.

<u>Error nine</u>: He loves *go* on long walks.

<u>Error</u>: after certain verbs we need to use the gerund. '**Love**' is a verb of feeling, and so is followed by the gerund.

<u>Correction</u>: He loves **going** on long walks.

<u>Notes</u>: We can also use the infinitive after the verbs of feeling, '**love**', '**like**', and '**hate**' but the meaning changes.

<u>Examples</u>: I love <u>reading</u> = this makes me very happy.

I love <u>to read</u> before I go to bed = this focuses on the time I love to read. There is no indication that I have 'a passion for reading'.

I like <u>eating</u> = when I eat I am happy.

I like <u>to eat</u> early in the evening = for me it is a good idea not to eat late. This does not mean that 'eating' is a passion of mine. These subtle differences should be noted by non natives of the English language in order to sound more like a 'native'

Exercise two

There are fourteen errors in the following passage. Find them and correct them then check your answers at the end of the exercise.

My mother's a secretary to a legal studio. She work part-time from 9 a.m. until 1 p.m. She travel to work with bus. My father's self employed; that means that he work for himself. He have a graphic design studio. Three peoples work for him. He work from 9 p.m. until 7 p.m. He has many work.

I and my sister study. We go both to the local secondary school. I love the geography. It is my favourite subject. I am in second year and my sister is in fourth year. The our school is a ten minutes walk from our house, so we don't need to use public transport for to get there.

Check your answers

Error one: My mother's a secretary **to** a legal studio.

Error: the use of the wrong preposition. We only use the preposition '**to**' with 'action verbs/motion verbs'.

Correction: My mother's a secretary **in** a legal studio.

Error two: She **work** part-time from 9 a.m. until 1 p.m.

Error: there is no '**s**' on the verb in third person singular.

Correction: She work**s** part-time from 9 a.m. until 1 p.m.

Notes: Students must remember that in the present tense, the 's' on the verb in third person **is vital**. It is one of the worst errors when the subject and verb do not agree.

Error three: She **travel** to work **with** bus.

4

Error: double error. There is no 's' on the verb and the student used the wrong preposition. We use the preposition '**by**' for means of transport.

Correction: She travel**s** to work **by** bus.

Error four: My father's self employed; that means that he *work* for himself.

Error: once again the student has failed to include the 's' on the verb '**work**', which is extremely important in third person singular in the present tense. It is an unforgivable error.

Correction: My father's self employed; that means that he work**s** for himself.

Error five: He *have* a graphic design studio.

Error: another error in third person singular in the present tense. This is highlighted in the book due to the fact that it is one of the most common and worst errors imaginable.

Correction: He **has** a graphic design studio.

Error six: Three *peoples* work for him.

Error: '**people**' is already plural. It is the irregular plural of '**person**' so there is no need to add an '**s**'.

Correction: Three **people** work for him.

Error seven: He *work* from 9 p.m. until 7 p.m.

Error: again the student has forgotten the '**s**' on third person singular of the verb in the present tense.

Correction: He **works** from 9 p.m. until 7 p.m.

Error eight: He has *many* work.

Error: '**work**' is an uncountable noun. We use '**many**' with countable nouns.

Correction: He has **a lot of** work. '**A lot of**' can be used with countable and uncountable nouns. We can also use '**much**' with uncountable nouns but it is more common in the negative-e.g. he **doesn't have much work**. In the positive, '**much + uncountable noun**' is more common in scientific writings or extremely formal English so be extra careful when using '**much**'.

Error nine: *I and my* sister study.

Error: if you place yourself at the beginning of a sentence or an utterance, use '**me** and my sister'. If you place yourself at the end then use, my sister and **I**'.

Error ten: We go *both* to the local secondary school.

Error: '**both**' is in the wrong position. Use '**both**' *before* the main verb but *after* the verb '**be**'.

Correction: We **both** go to the local secondary school.

With the verb '**be**'. We are **both** at ...

Error eleven: I love *the* geography.

Error: the use of the definite article '**the**', is not required when speaking or writing about school subjects.

Correction: I love Geography.

Error twelve: *The* our school.

Error: the definite article '**the**' is not required before possessive adjectives.

Correction: Our school.

Error thirteen: A ten minute*s* walk from our house.

Error: adjectives and adjective forms do not take the plural. '**Ten minute**' = two nouns. Although they are not adjectives, they become adjective forms which have the same function as an adjective, which is to describe a noun.

'What kind of walk?' A long walk, a short walk, a refreshing walk, a brisk walk or a ten minute walk.

'**Long**', '**short**', '**refreshing**' and '**brisk**' are adjectives and '**a ten minute**' is an adjective form.

Correction: A ten minute **walk** from our house.

Error fourteen: So we don't need to use public transport *for* to get there.

Error: the use of the preposition '**for**' is not used in English before an infinitive. It is used before a noun or adjective-noun combinations. This is known as the '**infinitive of purpose**', which is used when you '**give a reason**' for something.

E.g. **Why** do you use public transport? **To get** to school.

Why do you get up early? **To have** a shower.

Exercise three

There are twelve errors in the following passage. Find them and correct them then check your answers at the end of the exercise.

Our maternal grandparents live near to our house. My grandfather is English and my grandmother is German. We all go to Germany every summer. In fact, I speak a very good German. I have the cousins German. I use to play with them when I was a child and they spoke always to me in German. That's how I picked up it.

At lunchtime my mother and I eat to my grandmother's. My grandmother is a very good cooker. She is retired so she has a lot of free time to cook for we. My sister has the lunch at school. She prefers eat with her school friends.

Check your answers

Error one: Our maternal grandparents live near _**to**_ our house.

Error: the use of the preposition '**to**' after '**near**'. We say '**close to**' but '**near**'.

Correction: Our maternal grandparents live **near** our house.

Error two: We all go to _**the**_ Germany every summer.

Error: the definite article '**the**' is not used in English before the names of countries.

Correction: We all go to Germany every summer.

Error three: In fact, I speak _**a very good**_ German.

Error: do not use the indefinite article '**a**' to speak about a language.

8

Correction: In this case we can say, **my German is very good**. We use the adjective '**good**' to describe the noun '**German**'. In the above error, the student has used '**very good**' incorrectly. After the verb, in this case '**speak**' we need to use an adverb. Adverbs describe the verb they modify. We ask the question. 'How do you speak German?' 'Very well'. So the adverb from the adjective 'good', is '**well**'.

I speak German **well**.

I speak German **very well**. '**Very**' modifies adjectives and adverbs to give then a greater degree of intensity.

Error four: I have *the cousins German*.

Error: there is no need to use the definite article '**the**' because we are speaking about '**cousins**' in general and not specifically. There is also the error of placing the adjective (adjective of nationality in this case) after the noun instead of before it.

Correction: I have **German cousins**.

Error five: I *use* to play with them when I was a child.

Error: the student has forgotten to put a '**d**' on 'use'. This is a common error, also among native speakers of English due to the fact that '**use to**' and '**used to**', are pronounced in exactly the same way.

Correction: I **used** /ju:stu/to play with them when I was a child.

Note: When to use '**use to**'.

We use '**use to**' in the question as the auxiliary verb '**do**' takes the past tense and the verb remains in its infinitive form.

Did you **use** to /ju:stu/ play with your cousins when you were a child?

We also use '**use to**' in the negative with the auxiliary verb '**do**' taking the past tense in the form of '**did**'.

I didn't **use** to play with my cousins when I was a child.

Note: A reminder that '**use to**' is the past tense of the present simple. It is used to express past habits, past facts and states, just as in the same way the present simple is used to express present habits and facts or states.

Do not confuse '**use to**' with the verb '**use**'. They are two different things altogether.

Compare the pronunciation:

I use /juːz/

I use to /juːstu/

I used /juːzd/

I used to /juːstu/

Error six: They spoke *always* to me in German.

Error: the adverb of frequency '**always**' is in the wrong position in the sentence.

Correction: They **always** spoke to me in German.

Note: Remember that adverbs of frequency come *before* the main verb but always *after* the verb '**be**'.

Error seven: That's how I *picked up it*.

Error: with phrasal verbs, the object pronoun, in this case '**it**', can *never* be placed at the end.

Compare: I picked **German** up. I picked up **German**. I picked **it** up. I picked up it. (Wrong)

Note: **Pick** (something) **up** is a phrasal verb which is both *separable* and *inseparable*.

Error eight: At lunchtime my mother and I eat *to* my grandmother's.

Error: the preposition '**to**', as already mentioned previously, is used with motion verbs and not state verbs. '**Eat**' is a state verb. To understand if a verb is a motion verb, think about if the action moves from point A to point B, as in '**walk to**', '**run to**' etc. You walk from point A to point B. You run from point A to point B. '**Speak to**' is another example. You speak from point A (the speaker) to point B (the listener). '**At**' takes the place of '**to**' when the verb is motionless.

Correction: At lunchtime my mother and I eat **at** my grandmother's. (The apostrophe (') + (**s**) = at my grandmother's house. We do not need to write or say '**house**' as it is already understood.

Error nine**:** My grandmother is a very good *cooker.*

Error: it is common for learners of the English language to logically think of the noun '**cooker**' as a job. This is because many jobs end in '**er**', such as 'lawy**er**', 'teach**er**', 'bak**er**', 'butch**er**', etc. A **cooker** is a machine that you use to cook. The job is '**a cook**' and not '**a cooker**'.

Correction: My grandmother is a very good **cook**.

Error ten: She is retired so she has a lot of free time to cook for *we*.

Error: the use of the subject pronoun (we) as opposed to the object pronoun (us).

Correction: She is retired so she has a lot of free time to cook for **us**.

Note: Remember to use subject pronouns *before* the verb and object pronouns *after* the verb.

Error eleven: My sister has *the* lunch at school.

Error: do not use the definite article '**the**' or the indefinite articles '**a**' or '**an**' before '**breakfast**', '**lunch**' or '**dinner**', unless specifying one in particular.

Correction: My sister has lunch at school.

Note: An example of 'specifying' one particular breakfast, lunch or dinner is as follows:

The lunch we had in that small café was extremely good. In this example we are specifying a particular lunch.

Error twelve: She prefers *eat* with her school friends.

Error: after the verb '**prefer**', we need to use the infinitive with the '**to**' or the gerund. '**Prefer**' is one of those verbs which takes both the infinitive or the gerund when another verb follows it.

Correction: She prefers **to** eat with her school friends or she prefers **eating** with her school friends.

Exercise four

There are fifteen errors in the following passage. Find them and correct them then check your answers at the end of the exercise.

Free time

In my free time I read the books. I love Harry Potter. At the moment I reading 'Harry Potter and the Goblet of Fire'. J.K. Rowling is my preferred writer. She has a great ability. It is four years that I read books by J.K. Rowling. I like her books because she writes very clear so the stories are easy to follow. My mother and my sister read them also. My father is not interesting in them. He does not like read. He spends his free time to design things on the computer. That is his passion. After all, he is a graphic designer.

I play a lot of sports too. Every Monday, after school, I do swimming. I like music too. I play piano and I have piano lessons two times a week. We have the beautiful piano in my living room.

Check your answers

Error one: In my free time I read *the* books.

Error: the use of '**the**' is not required for general information.

Correction: In my free time I read books.

Notes: As previously mentioned, use '**the**' when specifying and not when generalising.

Example: I read **the** books that my mother bought me. Here we specify '**which**' books. ***The ones** my mother bought me.

*Use '**the ones**' so as not to repeat the noun. Use '**the one**' to substitute singular nouns and '**the ones**' to substitute plural nouns.

E.g. Which book? **The one** (= the book) my mother bought me. Which books? **The ones** (= the books) my mother bought me.

Error two: At the moment *I reading* 'Harry Potter and the Goblet of Fire'.

Error: '**at the moment**' indicates something in progress now so the use of the present continuous is required. Many students forget that the present continuous is formed with the verb '**be**' + **the gerund** of the required verb. Without the verb '**be**', the above phrase is ungrammatical. This is a common error among lower level learners of the English language.

Correction: At the moment I **am** reading 'Harry Potter and the Goblet of Fire'.

Contracted form: I'**m** reading.

Error three: J.K. Rowling is my *preferred* writer.

Error: the use of an invented adjective due to mother tongue interference from the student. This is. The adjective the student is looking for is '**favourite**'.

Correction: J.K. Rowling is my **favourite** writer.

Error four: She *has a great ability*.

Error: the above sentence is grammatically correct but very uncommon among native speakers.

Correction: She is very talented.

Error five: *It is four years that I read* books by J.K. Rowling.

Error: the above sentence does not impede understanding but it is not the type of utterance you would hear from a native speaker of English.

Correction: I **have been reading** books by J.K. Rowling **for** four years.

Notes: The use of the '**<u>present perfect continuous</u>**' is the natural way for native speakers.

<u>Frequently asked student questions</u>

Q. How do I remember when to use the present perfect continuous?

A. If you already understand that the present continuous 'I am reading' indicates an action in progress at the moment of speaking, then the present perfect continuous is not so difficult. The present perfect continuous (when used with '**<u>for</u>**' and '**<u>since</u>**') indicates an action that was in continuous before the present moment and is still continuing now-in the present.

I am reading (now) in progress

Remove the verb '**<u>be</u>**', in this case '**<u>am</u>**', and replace it with '**<u>have been</u>**'.

I ~~am~~ **have been** reading J.K. Rowling books **<u>for</u>** four years.

Four years ago I started and I am still reading them.

Notes: We **_cannot_** use the **<u>present continuous</u>** to refer to anything that was in progress **_<u>before</u>_** this moment. That is why the present perfect continuous is an important tense. It links an action in progress in the past and extends it into the present and possibly also into the future.

If you remember the grammatical meaning of '**<u>perfect</u>**', then you cannot go wrong. '**<u>Perfect</u>**' = before now. Present (perfect) continuous = the present continuous with the (perfect) added making it a 'before now action that continues and is still in progress at the moment of speaking'.

<u>Error six</u>: She writes very **_clear_**.

<u>Error</u>: '**<u>clear</u>**' is an adjective so it is used to describe a noun. Here the student has used it as an adverb to describe the verb '**<u>write</u>**'.

<u>Correction</u>: She writes very **<u>clearly</u>**. The adverb from the adjective '**<u>clear</u>**' is '**<u>clearly</u>**'. Many adverbs derive from adjectives and many of them end in '**<u>ly</u>**'.

Notes: To understand whether you have to use an adverb, then ask yourself the question, 'how does someone do something?' **How** does she write? She writes **clearly**. For adjectives you need to ask yourself the question, '**what kind of** writer is she?' 'She's a **clear** writer'. '**Clear**' is the adjective that describes the noun '**writer**'.

Error seven: My mother and my sister read them *also*.

Error: the wrong positioning of '**also**'.

Correction: My mother and sister **also** read them = not only do I read Harry Potter books but my mother and sister read them as well/too.

Error eight: My father is not *interesting* in them.

Error: the use of an '**ing**' adjective instead of an '**ed**' adjective.

Correction: My father is not **interested** in them.

Notes: There are many adjectives in English known as '**ed**' and '**ing**' adjectives. The '**ed**' adjectives are the same as past participles of regular verbs. The '*ing*' adjectives look like '**gerunds**'.

The choice of which one to use depends on whether it is something we feel or not.

My father is not **interested** is correct because the '**ed**' adjectives indicate a feeling. This means that he has **no interest in something**.

If we say, '**my father is not interesting**', then the meaning changes. It means that **my father is a boring person**, so be careful when using those adjectives.

Error nine: He does not like *read*.

Error: this is the same error seen previously.

Correction: He does not like **reading**. (Reading does not give him pleasure)

We need the gerund after verbs of feelings to imply '**in general**'.

Error ten: He spends his free time *to design* things on the computer.

Error: the use of the infinitive instead of the gerund.

Correction: He spends his free time **designing** things on the computer.

Notes: Spend time (**doing**) something – spend time + **gerund**

Error eleven: I *play* a lot of sports too.

Error: wrong verb – the use of the verb '**play**' instead of '**do**'.

Correction: I **do** a lot of sports too.

Notes: If an individual sport is a noun, such as tennis, then we can say, I **play** tennis.

If an individual sport is a verb, then we use **go** + **gerund of the verb**.

E.g. The verb '**swim**' becomes 'I go swimming'. The verb '**run**' becomes 'I **go** running'. The verb '**ski**' becomes 'I **go** skiing'.

As always, English has several exceptions to the general rule which are: **do** karate, **do** judo, **do** yoga, **do** aerobics.

Error twelve: Every Monday, after school, I *do* swimming.

Correction: I **go** swimming, as explained in the notes following '**error eight**'.

Error thirteen: I play piano.

Error: we use '**the**' for all musical instruments when using the verb '**play**'. You play the piano, the violin, the guitar, the flute, etc.

Correction: I play **the** piano.

Error fourteen: I have piano lessons *two times* a week.

Error: we say, once, twice, three times, four times, five times, six times, etc. You only need to remember that the first two are different.

Correction: I have piano lessons **twice** a week.

Error fifteen: We have *the* beautiful piano in our living room.

Error: the use of the definite article '**the**' instead of the indefinite article '**a**'. We are not specifying a particular piano so '**the**' cannot be used. An example of specifying a particular piano is: **The** piano in that shop window is the one I want to buy. (In this example a particular piano is referred to)

Exercise five

<u>**Free time**</u> (cont...)

There are ten errors in the following passage. Find them and correct them then check your answers at the end of the exercise.

I not watch TV a lot but I play computer games when I want relax. This strengthens my concentration. I also make many photographs when I have some free time and upload them to facebook. I am very good in photography. It is possible that one day I will become a professional photographer, at least I hope yes.

Last christmas my mother buyed me a very good camera and I made a lot of photos on christmas day.

Check your answers

Error one: I *not* watch TV a lot.

<u>Error</u>: in the present simple we use '<u>**do not**</u>' contracted to '<u>**don't**</u>' when we make sentences in the negative in first person singular (I), second person singular (you), first person plural (we), second person plural (you) and third person plural (they). However, in the negative of third person singular, that is, <u>**he**</u>, <u>**she**</u>, <u>**it**</u>, '<u>**do not**</u>' changes to '<u>**does not**</u>' contracted to '<u>**doesn't**</u>'. Remember that in the negative, the verb 'loses' the '<u>**s**</u>' due to the fact that the '<u>**s**</u>' is now on 'doe<u>s</u>'. E.g. he eat<u>s</u>/he doe<u>s</u>n't eat.

<u>Correction</u>: I <u>**don't**</u> watch TV a lot.

<u>Error two</u>: I play computer games when I *want relax*.

<u>Error</u>: if another verb follows the verb '<u>**want**</u>' then it needs to be in the infinitive with the '<u>**to**</u>'.

19

Correction: I play computer games when I want **to** relax.

Error three: I also **make** many photographs when I have some free time and upload them to facebook.

Error: the use of the wrong verb. '**Make**' a photograph would imply, constructing one with your hands.

Correction: I also **take** many photographs.

Error four: I am very good *in* photography.

Error: the use of the wrong preposition.

Correction: I am very good **at** photography.

Error five: *It is possible* that one day I will become a professional photographer.

Error: although this is not grammatically incorrect, it is not what a native speaker would use. It is clear to see that it has been written by someone who is foreign to the English language. In order to become more proficient in English, it is important to learn '**standard English**', that is, the English that is spoken by the natives.

Correction: I **might become** a professional photographer one day.

Notes: English is a concise language and *less* is *more*, so to speak. The fewer words you use the better. '**It is possible that one day I will become a professional photographer**' has twelve words, whereas '**I might become a professional photographer one day**', has only eight words. 'The modal auxiliary verb '**might**' does the job of expressing possibility as does '**may**' which is a more formal version of '**might**', therefore it is the better choice.

Error six: At least I hope *yes*.

Error: use 'so' and not 'yes' after the verb 'hope'.

Correction: At least I hope **so**.

Notes: After certain verbs, usually verbs which express some degree of '**uncertainty**', '**so**' is used to avoid *repetition*.

Do you think it'll rain tomorrow? I hope **so** = I hope *it will rain*.

Do you think she'll be late? I expect **so** = I expect *she will be late*.

Is Jane coming to the party? I believe **so** = I believe *she is coming*.

Is John at work? I think so = I think *he is at work*. '**Think**' is weaker than '**believe**' which carries a stronger assumption.

Should we go now? I suppose **so** = I suppose *we should go*. '**Suppose**' carries a weaker assumption than '**think**' and '**believe**'.

Error seven: Last *c*hristmas

Error: Christmas should begin with a capital letter. English has rigid rules about punctuation. Feast days, such as **C**hristmas, **E**aster and **N**ew **Y**ear, should all be capitalised.

Error eight: My mother *buyed* me a very good camera.

Error: the student has thought that '**buy**' is a regular verb, when it is in fact, irregular.

Correction: My mother **bought** me a very good camera. Buy/**bought**/bought

Notes: Irregular verbs should be memorised, at least seven each day, and example sentences should be written in a note book. The path to speaking correct English is narrow. There is no quick route. How the student organises his/her studies is vital for a good outcome. Teachers and course books are guides but what the student does is of utmost importance. Teachers cannot memorise anything for the student, nor can they wave a magic wand. There are no magic formulas - it is the diligent student who reaps the rewards.

Error nine: I *made* a lot of photos.

Error: the use of the wrong verb.

Correction: I **took** a lot of photos.

Notes: It is important to become familiar with verb + noun collocations, that is, which verb is used with different nouns.

E.g. **make** breakfast, **take** photos, **have** lunch, **have** a shower, etc.

Error ten: On *christmas* day.

Error: this is a punctuation error, see notes for 'error seven'.

Correction: On **C**hristmas day.

Exercise Six

<u>**Last New Year**</u>

There are ten errors in the following passage. Find them and correct them then check your answers at the end of the exercise.

Let me to tell you of how I passed last New Year. My parents allowed me go to a street party in the town centre with my friends. I and my friends had a great time. We ate salmon sandwiches and drunk apple cider. We listened music and danced. At midnight we said goodbye to the old year and welcomed the new one. We each did a New Year's resolution, that is, a promise to do or not to do something. At one o'clock in the night we made our way home. My parents and grandparents were still up so we all kissed and hugged and wished ourselves a happy and prosperous coming year.

Check your answers

<u>Error one</u>: Let me **to** tell you ...

<u>Error</u>: the use of the infinitive with the '**to**'

<u>Correction</u>: Let me tell you.

<u>Notes</u>: 'Make' (force) and 'Let' (allow), take the bare infinitive (without 'to') when used with another verb.

<u>Error two</u>: How I **passed** last New Year.

<u>Error</u>: the wrong choice of verb.

<u>Correction</u>: How I **spent** last New Year.

<u>Error four</u>: My parents **allowed me go** to a street party.

23

Error: after '**allow**' we need the infinitive with the '**to**'. Allow (someone) **to do** (something) = give someone your permission to do something.

Correction: My parents allowed me **to** go to a street party.

Error five: *I and* my friends had a great time.

Error: as seen in a previous error, if you mention yourself at the beginning of the sentence or utterance, say '**me and my friends**'. If you mention yourself at the end, say, '**my friends and I**'.

Error six: We ate salmon sandwiches and *drunk* apple cider.

Error: the use of the past participle instead of the past simple tense.

Correction: We ate salmon sandwiches and **drank** apple cider.

Notes: Since this is a common error, it is a good idea to remember the following pattern.

With irregular verbs such as; drink-drank-drunk, sink-sank-sunk, ring-rang-rung, sing-sang-sung, stink-stank-stunk, normally have an (**i**) in the infinitive, an (**a**) in the past tense, and a (**u**) in the past participle.

However, although this is the general pattern, keep in mind that English is a language full of exceptions to any general rule as seen in the following verb pattern.

Sting-stung-stung

Error seven: We *listened music* and danced.

Error: a common error among non natives is to forget to use the preposition '**to**' after the verb '**listen**'. You listen **to** someone or something.

Correction: We listened **to** music and danced.

Error eight: We each *did* a New Year's resolution, that is, a promise either to do or not to do something.

Error: the use of the wrong verb.

Correction: We each **made** a New Year's resolution.

Notes: **Verb/noun collocations** are an important part of English. They need to be learned to increase proficiency and to sound more like a native speaker. Constant exposure to the English language is fundamental in order to pick those collocations up.

Error nine: At one o'clock in the *night* we made our way home.

Error: some languages use the expression 'one o'clock at night/or in the night', but after midnight, the English language uses 'in the morning'.

Correction: At one o'clock in the **morning** we made our way home.

Error ten: My parents and grandparents *were still up so we all kissed and hugged and wished *ourselves* a happy and prosperous coming year. *To be still up = not to be in bed yet.

Error: confusion between '**each other**' and '**reflexive pronouns**'.

Correction: My parents and grandparents were still up so we all kissed and hugged and wished **each another** a happy and prosperous coming year.

Notes: '**Each other**' is a reciprocal pronoun and is used when person **A** does something to person **B** and person **B** does the same to **A**. They reciprocate.

I wished my parents a happy and prosperous coming year and my parents wished me a happy and prosperous coming year = we wished each other a happy and prosperous new year.

The reflexive pronouns, myself, yourself, himself, herself, itself, ourselves, yourselves, themselves = A does something to A, which means that the subject and the object are the same person or thing.

E.g. **I** bought **myself** a Christmas present. '**I**' and '**myself**' is the same person.

The cat is washing **itself**.

Notes: We also use the reflexive pronouns preceded with '**by**', are used to indicate that a person does something alone without anyone else.

E.g. **I** live **by myself** = nobody else lives with me, I live alone.

She always eats **by herself** = she eats alone.

The child plays **by himself** = he plays alone.

I don't need any help. **I** can do it **by myself** = I am able to do it alone.

Exercise seven

- -

My pets

There are four errors in the following passage. Find them and correct them then check your answers at the end of the text.

Hello. My name's Rolf and I live in a big house with a big garden. The house is more bigger than the one we lived in until last year. My father bought the house because it had such nice garden which is perfect for my pets.

I have a dog named Redford and I also have three cats named Pinky, Perky and Porky. Porky is called Porky because he is fat. He eats a lot. He is the most fat cat I have ever seen. I haven't a rabbit but I want one for my birthday which is next month. There's a large rabbit's hutch in the garden which was already there when we came to live in this house.

Check your answers

Error one: The house is **_more bigger_** than the one we lived in until last year.

Error: double comparative.

Correction: The house is **bigger** than the one we lived in until last year.

Notes: A common error is to put '**more**' before a comparative adjective that is already in the comparative form.

Remember to add '**er**' at the end of adjectives with one syllable. '**Big**' has one syllable. Double the final consonant if **_one_** vowel precedes it. Big + g + er.

Add '**more**' to adjectives with two syllables or more.

E.g. **more** im-por-tant.

27

Adjectives which end in '**y**' are counted as one-syllable adjectives. Change the '**y**' into '**i**' and add '**er**'.

E.g. nois**y**-nois**ier**, busy-bus**ier**, hungr**y**-hungr**ier**, angr**y**-angr**ier**.

Error two: My father bought the house because it had *such nice* garden which is perfect for my pets.

Error: use 'such + a + adjective + noun'.

Correction: My father bought the house because it had such **a** nice garden.

Error three: He is the *most fat* cat I have ever seen.

Error: this is a superlative adjective error.

Correction: He is the fatt**est** cat I have ever seen.

To form the superlative, always use '**the** + **one syllable adjective** + **est**' and double the final consonant if one vowel precedes it.

F-**a**-t–**one vowel** precedes the final consonant '**t**' so double the '**t**' and add **est**.

For longer adjectives use '**the** + **most** + **adjective**'

E.g. **the most** important.

If the adjective ends in '**y**' then change the '**y**' into '**i**' and add '**est**'.

E.g. Happ**y** – happ**iest**.

Error four: I *haven't* a rabbit but I want one for my birthday which is next month.

Error: the wrong negative.

Correction: I **don't have** a rabbit or I **haven't got** a rabbit.

<u>Notes</u>: The verb '**have**' has two functions in the English language. It functions as a **<u>full verb</u>** and also as an **<u>auxiliary verb</u>**. As an auxiliary verb it can be made negative. As a full verb it can't.

Let's compare '**have**' as an auxiliary and '**have**' as a full verb.

I **have** a cat. (Full verb)

<u>Negative</u>

1. I **<u>don't</u>** have a cat (full verb requires the auxiliary '**<u>do</u>**' to form the negative in the present simple)

2. I **haven't** got a cat ('**have**' as an auxiliary verb which aids the verb '**<u>got</u>**' in the negative)

With the present perfect, '**have**' is an auxiliary verb used with a main verb in its past participle form.

I **haven't been** to London.

The main verb is '**<u>been</u>**' and the auxiliary verb is '**have**'. Only auxiliary verbs are made negative.

In the past simple tense the verb requires the past tense of the auxiliary verb '**<u>do</u>**' to form the negative.

I *hadn't* a dog (Incorrect as there is no other verb present, without another verb, have is a full verb and not an auxiliary)

I **didn't have** a dog (Correct)

Note that '**<u>have got</u>**' is only used in the present tense to indicate possession. The past tense of '**<u>have got</u>**', is not '**<u>hadn't got</u>**', but '**<u>didn't have</u>**'.

Exercise eight

<u>The boyfriend of my sister</u>

There are eighteen errors in the following passage. Find them and correct them then check your answers at the end.

The boyfriend of my sister is quiet a nice person but he has one fault. He is jealous and possessive and he often gets angry really easily. In fact sometime I see him become too much angry for silly things. He says it is because he has a stressful work.

He's a very good looking boy. He has got curly brown short hair and a beautiful smile. He is tall 1m 78 cm and has an athletic structure.

She knew him at a birthday party last summer and he felt in love with her instantly. They are together now for about a year.

She would like leave him but every time she tells him so he goes crazy. He always asks to her to give him one more occasion.

My sister tells to me that if he wouldn't be so angry and jealous, she would marry him as he has many other good qualities. He works very hardly and is well respected in the company where he works.

Hopefully he will change so that they can stay together but I doubt it. As the saying goes, 'a leopard cannot change its spots'.

<u>Error one</u>: ***The boyfriend of my sister***.

<u>Error</u>: we need to use the genitive case here.

<u>Correction</u>: My sister<u>'s</u> boyfriend.

<u>Error two</u>: He is ***quiet*** a nice person but he has one fault.

<u>Error</u>: the student has written '**<u>quiet</u>**' instead of '**<u>quite</u>**'.

<u>Correction</u>: He is **<u>quite</u>** a nice person.

<u>Notes</u>: This is a common error seeing that those two words look alike and sound quite alike. '**<u>Quiet</u>**' is an adjective and is the opposite of '**<u>noisy</u>**' while '**<u>quite</u>**' modifies an adjective.

On a scale

Very nice = a lot

Really nice = a lot

Quite nice = 50/50

We use '**<u>quite</u>**' before an adjective and '**<u>quite a</u>**' before an adjective + noun.

<u>Error three</u>: He is jealous and possessive and he gets ***often*** angry really easily.

<u>Error</u>: the adjective of frequency is in the wrong position in the sentence.

<u>Correction</u>: He **<u>often</u>** gets angry really easily.

<u>Notes</u>: A reminder that adjectives of frequency come ***before*** the main verb but ***after*** the verb '**<u>be</u>**'. There are exceptions with '**<u>sometimes</u>**' which can come at the beginning of a sentence or before the verb but always after the verb '**<u>be</u>**'.

<u>Error four</u>: In fact ***sometime*** I see him become ...

31

Error: '**sometime**' instead of '**sometimes**'.

Correction: In fact **sometimes** I see him become ...

Notes: **Some time** (two words) = an unspecified moment.

E.g. I'll see you **some time** = the time is not specified as no definite time has been set between person A and person B.

Error five: I see him become *too much* angry for silly things.

Error: '**too much**' instead of '**very**'.

Correction: I see him become **very** angry for silly things or I see him become **too** angry.

Notes: '**Too much**' is used before uncountable nouns and means '**in excess**'.

'**Too many**' is used before countable nouns and means '**in excess**'.

'**Too**' is used with adjectives to mean '**in excess**'.

In the above example (of the error) a person can becomes **very** angry (a lot) or **too angry** (excessively).

Error six: He says it is because he has a stressful *work*.

Error: the student used '**work**' instead of '**job**'.

Correction: He says it is because he has a stressful **job**.

Notes: '**Work**' is uncountable and '**job**' is countable. '**Job**' = profession. The use of the indefinite article '**a**' before the adjective '**stressful**' is an indicator that a singular countable noun will follow.

Error seven: He has got *curly brown short* hair and a beautiful smile.

Error: wrong adjective order.

Correction: He has got **short**, **brown**, **curly** hair.

<u>Notes</u>: The order of adjectives is as follows:

Determiner + opinion/fact + **size** + age + **colour** + nationality + **material** + qualifier + **noun**

Short (fact), **brown** (colour), **curly** (qualifier) **hair** (noun)

<u>Error eight</u>: He is *tall* 1m 78.

<u>Error</u>: He is 1m 78 tall.

<u>Error nine</u>: ... and has an athletic *structure*.

<u>Error</u>: '**structure**' is not used for people.

<u>Correction</u>: He has an athletic **build**.

<u>Error ten</u>: She *knew* him at a birthday party.

<u>Error</u>: the use of the wrong verb.

<u>Correction</u>:

(1) She **met** him at a birthday party. (She didn't know him before that moment). To meet is the initial physical encounter, then after that you can say you '**know someone**'.

(2) I **met** your sister last night. I hadn't seen her for a few years. (Encounter/see someone you already know)

<u>Notes</u>:

Meet (1) = become acquainted with (see someone and speak for the first time)

Meet (2) = fix an appointment to see a person you already know or casually encounter someone you already know.

<u>Error eleven</u>: He *felt* in love with her instantly.

<u>Error</u>: the use of the wrong past tense.

Correction: He **fell** in love with her instantly.

Notes: Common errors in English are getting confused between the irregular verbs 'fall/fell/fallen, and feel/felt/felt'.

Error twelve: ***They are together now for about a year***.

Error: we need to use the present perfect to join the past to the present.

Correction: They **have been** together **for** about a year.

Notes: Without the use of '**for**' and '**since**' the present perfect is used to indicate something that was completed before the present moment with no focus on time.

E.g. I've seen that film many times. (***Before now***-the time is of no relevance to the speaker)

When the time is relevant, use the past simple

E.g. I **saw** that film **last year**.

Error thirteen: She would ***like leave*** him but every time she tells him so he goes crazy.

Error: omission of '**to**' as part of the infinitive.

Correction: She would like **to** leave him.

Notes: If another verb follows '**would like**', it takes the infinitive with the '**to**'.

Error fourteen: He always asks ***to*** her to give him ...

Error: the use of the preposition '**to**' when it is not required.

Correction: He always asks her to give her ...

Notes: Ask (someone) to do something

Error fifteen: To give him one more ***occasion***.

Error: the use of the wrong noun.

Correction: He always asks her to give him one more **chance**.

Error sixteen: My sister tells *to* me

Error: the use of the preposition '**to**' with the verb '**tell**' when it is not required.

Correction: My sister tells me.

Notes: Tell (someone) something/tell (someone) to do something

Error seventeen: If he *wouldn't be* so angry and jealous, she would marry him as he has many other good qualities.

Error: double use of 'would + infinitive'

Correction: If he **weren't** so angry and jealous, she would marry him.

Notes: When forming the second conditional, used for hypothetical situations, the past tense is used after the '**if**' clause, (the condition) and '**would + infinitive**' are used on the result of the condition. A common error is to use '**would + infinitive**' after the '**if**' clause. This should be avoided or students risk losing marks in exams.

Error eighteen: He works very *hardly* and is well respected in the company where he works.

Error: the use of '**hardly**' instead of '**hard**'.

Correction: He works very **hard**.

Notes: This is a common error as students begin to learn that by putting '**ly**' at the end of an adjective we form an adverb. They are thinking logically when doing so. While it is true that this is often the case, the adjective '**hard**', is one of the several '**irregular**' adjectives. If the adjective is irregular, then the adverb is too. The adverb form of '**hard**' is the same as the adjective, that is, it remains as '**hard**'.

'**Hardly**' on the other hand, is an adverb of frequency.

<u>On a scale</u>: **Never** = 0%, **hardly** (**ever**) = more or less 3%, **occasionally** = about 7%, **sometimes** = about 20%, **often** = about 70% and **always** = 100%.

As you can see, '**hardly**' (which is also used with '**ever**') has a similar meaning to '**rarely**'.

He **hardly** works = almost zero.

He works **hard** = he works a lot.

As you can see, this error really impedes understanding as the listener or reader could misunderstand and think that the person rarely works when in fact he works a lot.

Exercise nine

My birthday party

There are twenty five errors in the following passage. Find them and correct them then check your answers at the end of the passage.

I did a great party last Saturday night at my parent's holiday house on the sea. Much of my friends were invited but they not all came. My friend Mandy said me that she didn't come because she didn't have nothing to wear. My friend Tony also didn't come because his car was broken down the day before the party and he had no idea how to arrive to the sea without his car. He said he couldn't come with the bus because where he lives there are no direct buses to our beach house, so at the end he decided to don't come. I told him that my brother could pick him up if he would have told me.

Two of my friends arrived lately because they lost themselves and another my friend must took a taxi when his motorbike broke.

Anyway, apart from that, it was a great party and twenty eight of the my friends came. We ate many foods and drank wine and beer and danced all night. We loved a lot the music which my brother's friend, who is a deejay, chose.

My friends all gave to me the very nice presents but the one I like the best was a silver beautiful photo frame with a picture of all us together.

Error one: I *did* a great party last Saturday night

Error: the use of the wrong verb.

Correction: I **had** a great party.

Error two: At my parent*'s* holiday house.

Error: the apostrophe is in the wrong position.

Correction: At my parent**s'** holiday house.

Notes: '**Parents**' consist of two people-mother and father. The plural genitive case has the apostrophe (') outside the '**s**'.

Examples

The boy**'s** house = the house of one boy.

The boy**s'** house = the house of more than one boy.

Error three: House *on* the sea.

Error: the use of the wrong preposition.

Correction: House **by** the sea.

Notes: House **by** the sea = **next to** the sea. **On** the sea = the house has the sea **under** it.

House on the sea (the sea is under the house)

Error four: **Much** of my friends were invited.

Error: the use of '**much**' instead of '**many**'.

Correction: **Many** of my friends were invited.

Notes: Remember to use '**much**' with uncountable nouns and '**many**' with countable nouns.

Error five: But they **not all came**.

Error: error in using the past tense negative.

Correction: But they didn't all come.

Notes: Remember that in the past simple tense, the auxiliary '**do**', used in the present simple, takes the past tense '**did**' and is used in past tense questions and negatives. The verb remains in its infinitive form.

Error six: My friend Mandy said **me** that ...

Error: the use of a direct object after the verb '**say**'.

Correction: My friend Mandy said that she didn't come ...

Notes: We use objects pronouns directly after the verb '**tell**' but not after '**say**'.

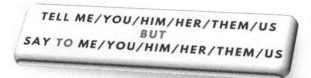

TELL ME/YOU/HIM/HER/THEM/US
BUT
SAY TO ME/YOU/HIM/HER/THEM/US

Error seven: She didn't come because she didn't have **nothing** to wear.

Error: the use of '**nothing**' when there already is a negative '**didn't**'.

Correction: She didn't come because she didn't have **anything** to wear.

Notes: Use '**anything**' in negatives. If you use '**nothing**' with a negative, it becomes a positive. In English, two negatives make a positive.

E.g. She didn't have **nothing** to wear = she had something to wear.

He didn't have **nothing** to say = he had something to say.

Error eight: My friend Tony also didn't come because his car *was* broken down the day before the party.

Error: the use of the auxiliary verb '**be**' instead of the auxiliary verb '**have**'.

Correction: My friend Tony also didn't come because his car **had** broken down the day before the party.

Notes: '**Had broken down**' = the past perfect. Use the past perfect for time shifts to show the sequence of events –the car broke down prior to the moment that he didn't come.

2. He **didn't come** (past tense)

1. His car **had broken down** (past perfect) – auxiliary verb '**have**' in its past tense form + the past participle of the verb.

The sequence of events is: 1) His car broke down. 2) He didn't come.

Error nine: He had no idea how to arrive *to* the sea without his car.

Error: the use of the wrong preposition.

Correction: He had no idea how to arrive **at** the sea without his car.

Notes: Remember to use '**to**' with verbs of movement/motion verbs and '**at**' for static verbs.

'**Arrive**' is a static verb.

You arrive **at** a place or a building.

You arrive **in** a town, city or country.

E.g. I arrived **at** the cinema at 7 p.m. but I went **to** the cinema at 7 p.m. '**Go**' is a motion verb so it requires the preposition '**to**'.

I arrived **in** New York late in the evening.

Error ten: He said he couldn't come *with the* bus because ...

Error: the use of the wrong preposition and the unnecessary use of the definite article '**the**'.

Correction: He said he couldn't come **by** bus because ...

Notes: We use the preposition '**by**' for means of transport.

By bus, **by** car, **by** plane, **by** taxi, **by** helicopter, **by** bicycle, **by** motorbike, **by** scooter *but* '**on** foot'.

If you come **with the** bus, it means that you and the bus come together so it completely changes the meaning rendering the utterance an absurdity.

Error eleven: ... so *at* the end ...

Error: the use of the wrong preposition.

Correction: ... so **in** the end ...

Notes: Much confusion is met when learners of English use '**in the end**' and '**at the end**'.

Frequently asked student questions

What is the difference?

The difference is that '**in the end**' = after discussing or thinking, you finally decide or agree to do something. It is similar in meaning to '**finally**'.

E.g. I didn't know which shoes to buy, but **in the end** I bought the black ones.

'**At the end**' = physically or metaphorically.

There is a supermarket **at the end** of our street. (Physical location)

At the end of the week I stop working and begin to relax. (When the week is finished)

At the end of the day, when you are in bed, think positive thoughts. This will help you sleep well and also it will help you wake up in a good mood. (When the day is finished)

At the end of the film we all stood up and left the cinema. (At the conclusion of the film)

At the end of the day we all leave work and go home. (When the day is finished)

At the end of the day, there is no harm in trying. (Idiomatic expression = when all is said and done)

At the end of the day, each man is responsible for his own happiness. (Idiomatic expression/when all is said and done)

Error twelve: ... he decided **to don't** come.

Error: the use of the wrong negative.

Correction: ... he decided **not to** come.

Notes: After certain verbs we use '**not**' to negate. '**Don't/doesn't**' are used to negate a primary verb, (in the present simple tense) in the case of the above example '**decide**' is the primary verb and '**come**' is the secondary verb.

I don't decide ... I decided **not** to

Error thirteen: I told him that my brother **could pick** him up if he **would have** told me.

Error: the student has tried to use the third conditional but made a mess of it.

Correction: I told him my brother **could have picked** him up if he **had told** me.

Notes: The third conditional refers to something in the past that did not happen.

It is formed by using 'if +subject + past perfect + subject + would/could/might + the present perfect structure.

E.g. I didn't see you yesterday so I didn't say hello.

= If I **had seen** you, I *would/could/might **have said** hello.

*The choice of the modal auxiliary verb depends on the level of certainty of the speaker.

I would have said hello (100%)

I could have said hello (I had this possibility)

I might have said hello (50% possibility)

Error fourteen: Two of my friends arrived *lately* ...

Error: the use of '**lately**' instead of '**late**'.

Correction: Two of my friends arrived **late**.

Notes: There is a logical explanation as to why students make this error. '**Late**' is an adjective but it is also an adverb. '**Lately**' looks like it is the adverb deriving from '**late**' but it isn't. It means '**recently**'. The reason this error is made is because students think logically and remember that very often when '**ly**' is added to an adjective, it makes the adjective become an adverb. So remember, that '**late**' is an adjective and also an adverb, while '**lately**' is only an adverb. Adjectives describe nouns, whereas the main function of an adverb is to modify a verb, although they are also used to modify adjectives and other adverbs. They tell us '**how**', '**when**' or '**where**' something happened.

Examples with '**lately**'

I haven't been sleeping well **lately** (in the reason past before this moment)

Have you seen any good films **lately**/recently?

Lately I've been eating too much.

Late as an adverb and as an adjective-two sentences with the same meaning:

He's always **late** for work. (Adverb which modifies '**is**')

He's a **late** time-keeper. (Adjective which modifies '**time-keeper**')

Error fifteen: ... because they *lost themselves* ...

Error: it is not possible for a person to lose him/herself. This would imply that **you** cannot find **you**, leading to an '**absurdity**'.

Correction: They got lost.

Notes: '**To get lost**' is reflexive

Error sixteen: ... and another *my friend* ...

Error: this is obviously a literal translation from the student's mother tongue.

Correction: ... and another **friend of mine**.

Notes: Say: a friend of **mine**, a friend of **yours**, a friend of **his**, a friend of **hers**, a friend of **ours**, a friend of **theirs**.

Error seventeen: ... *must took* a taxi ...

Error: the student has not mastered the use of modal verbs of deduction in the past.

Correction: ... must **have taken** ... used when we have strong reason to believe that something occurred before the present moment.

Notes: To remember the modal verbs of deduction in the past, think of '**must** + **present perfect**' to imply strong reason to assume something to be true, or '**could**/**might**/**may** + **present perfect**' to indicate a 50/50 possibility.

Error eighteen: ... when his motorbike *broke*.

Error: machinery, electrical or electronic devices usually '**break down**' which means, '**cease to function**'.

Correction: ... when his motorbike **broke down**.

Notes: '**Break down**' is one of the many commonly used phrasal verbs.

Error nineteen: ... anyway, apart from that, it was a great party and twenty eight of *the* my friends came.

Error: the use of the definite article '**the**' when it is not required.

Correction: ... anyway, apart from that, it was a great party and twenty eight of my friends came.

Notes: In English, never use an '**article**', be it definite or indefinite, before possessive adjectives.

Error twenty: We ate *many foods* and drank wine and beer and danced all night.

Error: '**food**' is uncountable. Uncountable nouns cannot be made plural and they cannot be preceded by '**many**' which is used exclusively with '**countable nouns**'.

Correction: We ate **a lot of** food ...

Notes: Although '**much**' is used with uncountable nouns, it more common in the negative and in the question. That is why it is safer to use '**a lot of**' as it can be used with both countable and uncountable nouns.

E.g. we **didn't** eat **much** food. How **much** food did you eat?

'**Much**' is very common in scientific or formal written English and in everyday English it is used a lot before '**more**' with comparative adjectives and nouns.

E.g. I earn **much more money** in this job than in my last.

The car is **much more expensive** than I thought it would be.

My son is **much taller** this year than what he was this time last year.

Error twenty one: We *loved a lot the music* which my brother's friend, who is a deejay, chose.

Error: the wrong sentence order.

Correction: We loved the music a lot.

Notes: Remember to use the **S**. **V**. **O**. formula in affirmative sentences, that is, '**s**ubject/**v**erb/**o**bject'.

Subject = we

Verb = loved

Object = the music

Extra information: to what degree = a lot.

Error twenty two: My friends all gave *to* me ...

Error: the use of the preposition '**to**' when it is not required.

Correction: My friends all gave me.

Notes: Give (someone) (something)

Give (something) to (someone)

Error twenty three: ... *the* very nice presents but ...

Error: the use of the definite article '**the**' when it is not required.

Correction: ... very nice presents

Error twenty four: ... the one I like the best *was* a ...

Error: inconsistency with the tenses.

Correction: ... the one I **like** best **is** *or* the one I **liked** best **was** ...

Error twenty five: ... a *silver beautiful* photo frame with a picture of all us together.

Error: the adjectives are in the wrong order.

Correction: ... a **beautiful silver** photo frame.

See page 33 for the order of English adjectives.

Exercise ten

My studies

There are thirteen errors in the following passage. Find them and correct them. The answers follow after the passage.

At the moment I study at the university. I am in the third year of my studies and I love the course. I'm studying biomedical engineering. This month I have been designing biomedical equipments and devices.

I have become interested to biomedical Engineering when my uncle lost one of his hands in a working accident when I had only twelve years old and my uncle had only thirty five. At the time of the accident my uncle worked in a field and his hands were caught in the axle of a tractor. Micro surgeons tried saving his hands but it was not possible.

It was a moment very terrible for our family but thanks to bio medics and there research, he now has prosthetic hands.

That was when I knew I had to help the other people like my uncle in the future so that is why I chose this path.

In my course I've studied biology and I've taken a lot of design classes. I've had the opportunity to watch surgical procedures because one day in the future I may have to design surgical tools.

Errors one and two: At the moment I *study* at *the* university.

Errors: '**at the moment**' is the signal phrase to indicate that something is in progress now, so we need to use the present continuous, 'subject + a version of the verb 'be' + gerund of the verb'. The use of the definite article '**the**' when it is not required.

Correction: At the moment I**'m studying** at university.

Notes: A reminder that we use '**the**' to specify.

An example of specification

I'm studying at **the** university in my town. Here we define '**which**' university. We refer to a specific one.

Error three: This month I have been designing biomedical *equipments* and devices.

Error: '**equipment**' is a non countable noun. It cannot be made plural.

Correction: This month I have been designing biomedical **equipment** and devices.

Errors three, four and five: I *have become* interested *to* biomedical Engineering when my uncle lost one of his hands in a *working accident* ...

Errors: the use of the present perfect with a past time reference (the '**when**' is indicated). The use of the wrong preposition. We say, 'interested **in**' (something or someone). 'A **working accident**' is not what a native speaker would say.

Correction: I **became** interested **in** biomedical engineering when my uncle lost both his hands in a **work-related** accident.

Error six: ... when I *had* only twelve years old and my uncle *had* only thirty five.

Error: The use of '**have**' when stating 'age' instead of '**be**'.

Correction: When I **was** only twelve years old and my uncle **was** only thirty five.

Errors seven and eight: At the time of the accident my uncle *worked* in a field and his hands were caught in the *tractor's axle*.

Errors: the use of the past simple instead of the past continuous (the action of working was in progress), the use of the genitive case for objects.

Correction: At the time of the accident my uncle **was working** in a field and his hands were caught in the **axle of the tractor**.

Notes: The genitive case is usually not used for 'objects'.

E.g. The table's legs (incorrect)–the legs of the table (correct)

Error nine: Micro surgeons tried *saving* his hand but *it was not possible.

Error: use of the gerund instead of the infinitive.

Correction: Micro surgeons tried **to save** his hands but *it was not possible.

*Although the phrase 'it was not possible' is grammatically correct, it is not what a native speaker would say in this context. Look at the more natural ways below.

Micro surgeons tried **to save** his hands but failed.

Micro surgeons tried **to save** his hands but were unsuccessful in their attempts.

Or better still, micro-surgeons made an attempt to re-attach his hands.

Notes: Try + infinitive = attempt/try + gerund = find a solution

Errors ten, eleven and twelve: It was *a moment very terrible* for our family but thanks to bio-medics and *there* research, he now has prosthetic hands.

Errors: the wrong word order and the unnatural use of 'moment', the use of '**very**' with an extreme adjective, and the use of '**there**' instead of the possessive adjective '**their**'.

Correction: It was a terrible **time** for our family but thanks to bio-medics and **their** research ...

Notes: With extreme adjectives, do not use '**very**'.

Examples of extreme adjectives

Normal (big)-Extreme (enormous) **very big** *but never* ~~very enormous~~ x

Normal (small)-Extreme (tiny) **very small** *but never* ~~very tiny~~ x

Normal (cold)-Extreme (freezing) **very cold** *but never* ~~very freezing~~ x

Normal (hot)-Extreme (boiling) **very hot** *but never* ~~very boiling~~ x

However, with extreme adjectives, we can use '**really**', and '**absolutely**'.

It was **absolutely boiling** on the beach today.

It was **really cold** this morning.

Error thirteen: That was when I knew I had to help *the other people* like my uncle in the future so I chose this path.

Error: instead of '**the other people**' it is more natural to say '**others**'. '**Others**' = other people. There is no need to use the definite article '**the**' either because we mean '**others**' **in general** without specifying exactly '**who**' they are.

Correction: That was when I knew I had to help **others** like my uncle in the future so that is why I chose this path.

Exercise eleven

Brighton and my host family

There are thirty errors in the following letter. Find them and correct them then check your answers at the end of the letter.

Dear mum and dad,

It's a week that I'm in Brighton. Mr and Mrs White took me from the airport in their car to their home. They are nice persons. Mrs White cook really well. I had afraid that the English food would not be good but so far I like. Mrs White's husband works in London so I don't see him very often. He comes to home in the evening tired and eats and goes to the bed.
They have a daughter Emily which is a year more young of me. She told to me that my English is good. I am so happy for this. I hope improve it during my stay.
I attend an English school every mornings. I am in the intermediate class. There are many other students from all of the world. Someone of them are from Japan and someone of them are from China. There is also some Italians and Spaniards. We speak each other in English.
I like Brighton. There is a lovely beach and there are many tourists. It is a bright and lively town and full of young people.
The weather it is sunny today but on Monday and Tuesday there was the rain. I hadn't an umbrella but my host family borrowed me one. Tomorrow if I will have time, I will take the photos of the family and the house I live in and send to you them.
Next Saturday Mrs White will take me to the large shopping centre in Churchill Square. She said me there are more than eighty shops. I want buy some English clothes.
Hope you and dad are well,
Speak to you soon,

lots of love,

Wendy .

Check your answers

Error one: **It's a week that I'm** in Brighton.

Error: from past to present use the '**present perfect**'.

Correction: **I've been in Brighton for a week**.

Error two: Mr and Mrs White **took me from** the airport in **their car** to their **home**.

Error: **too many words**. This is not what a native speaker would say.

Correction: Mr and Mrs White **drove me** from the airport to their **house**.

Error three: They are nice **persons**.

Error: the plural of '**person**' is '**people**'.

They are very nice **people**.

Notes: The plural form '**persons**' exists in English but it is used only in formal contexts such as on notice boards. You wouldn't hear it in everyday language.

Error four: Mrs White **cook** really well.

Error: no '**s**' on third person singular.

Correction: Mrs White cook**s** really well.

Errors five, six and seven: I **had** afraid that the English food **will** not be good but so far I like.

Errors: the use of the wrong verb. Use the verb '**be**'. To **be** afraid of (something or someone).

The use of '**will**' instead of '**would**'. After '**like**' the student has forgotten to use an object pronoun. 'Like (something or someone)

53

Correction: I **was** afraid that the English food **would** not be good but so far I like **it**. ('**it**' refers to the food)

Errors eight and nine: He comes *to* home in the evening tired and eats and goes to *the* bed.

Errors: although it is true that we use the preposition of movement '**to**' after '**motion**' verbs, there is an exception to the general rule with the noun '**home**'. 'Go home', 'come home', 'run home', etc.

We do not use the definite article '**the**' with '**go to bed**' unless specifying a particular bed.

E.g. He goes to **the** bed in the living room.

Correction: He comes home in the evening tired and eats and goes to bed.

Errors ten and eleven: They have a daughter Emily *which* is a year *more young of* me.

Errors: use '**who**' for '**people**' and '**which**' for things. '**That**' can be used for both people and things, although it is more grammatically correct to use '**who**' for people.

Remember that we add '**er**' to one syllable adjectives to make the comparisons and use '**than**' and not '**of**'.

Correction: They have a daughter Emily **who** is a year **younger than** me.

Error twelve: She told *to* me that my English is good.

Error: we don't use the preposition '**to**' directly after 'tell', as already seen previously. (Tell someone something) or (Tell something to someone)

Correction: She told me *that my English was good.

*The use of '**that**' is optional. We can also say: she told me my English was good.

An example of 'tell something to someone'

He told lies **to** me

Errors thirteen and fourteen: I am so happy *for* this. I *hope improve* it during my stay.

Error: the use of the wrong preposition. You can be happy **about something** but happy **for someone**. If we use another verb after the verb 'hope', then this verb takes the infinitive with the '**to**'.

Correction: I am so happy **about** this. I hope **to** improve it during my stay.

Error fifteen: I attend an English language school every morning**s**.

Error: '**every**' is used with **singular nouns**.

Correction: I attend an English language school every **morning**.

Error sixteen: There are many other students from all *of* the world.

Error: the use of the wrong preposition

Correction: There are many other students from all **over/around** the world.

Error seventeen: *Someone* of them are from Japan and *someone* of them are from China.

Error: '**someone**' refers to just one person. The student would like to express more than one.

Correction: **Some of them** are from Japan and **some** are from China. We do not need to repeat '**of them**' in the second part of the sentence. In fact the sentence can be written without '**of them**' without altering the meaning.

Some are from Japan and **some** are from China. (This is better – remember that in English, '**less**' is '**more**'.

Error eighteen and nineteen: There *is* also some Italians and Spaniards. We *speak each* other in English.

55

Error: the student has forgotten the preposition '**to**'. We speak '**to**' someone. He has also used the singular verb '**is**' after '**there**' instead of the plural verb '**are**'.

Correction: There **are** also some Italians and Spaniards. We speak **to** each other in English.

Errors twenty and twenty one: The weather *it* is sunny today but on Monday and Tuesday *there was* the rain.

Errors: the use of two subjects and the unnatural construction '**there was the rain**'.

Correction: **It** is sunny. (It is understood that the subject pronoun '**it**' refers to the weather). On Monday and Tuesday **it rained** or **it was raining**. There are two possibilities; or the **past simple** or the **past continuous**.

On Monday and Tuesday it was raining

Errors twenty two and twenty three: I *hadn't* an umbrella but my host family *borrowed* me one.

Errors: as seen previously, when the verb '**have**' is functioning as a '**full verb**', it needs the help of the auxiliary verb '**do**' or '**does**' (in third person singular) in the present simple tense to form the negative and question, and the auxiliary verb '**did**' (the past tense of '**do/does**') to form the negative and question in the past tense. The student has also got confused between the verbs '**borrow**' and '**lend**', which is a common error.

Correction: I didn't have an umbrella but my host family lent me one *or* lent one to me.

Notes: Remember that you borrow something **_from_** someone but you lend something **_to_** someone or you can lend someone something.

Example sentences

Can **I borrow** your car? (Can **I take** your car for a period?)

Can **you lend** your car to me? (Can **you give** me your car for a period?)

Errors twenty four, twenty five, twenty six and twenty seven: Tomorrow if I **_will_** have time, I will take **_the_** photos of the family and the house I **_live_** in and send **_to_** you them.

Error: after the '**if**' clause in the first condition, do not put '**will**'. The auxiliary verb '**will**' is only present in the result of the condition, that is, the second part of the sentence following the condition. There is no need to use the definite article '**the**' as in the above example the student is talking about photos in general and not specific ones.

'**I live**' is a permanent state. The student is with a host family for a set period so it is more appropriate to say '**the house I'm staying in**'. Remember that the present continuous has three uses in English.

1. An action in progress now ... I'm writing a letter (now)

2. Something in progress in this period ... I'm staying with the White family (only for this period of my life)

3. For a future arrangement when used with a future time clause ... I'm playing tennis tomorrow with my friend Albert.

Last of the errors: send **_to_** you them (the wrong order) 'send them to you or send you them' are the correct forms.

You send (something to someone) **_or_** you send (someone something).

Correction: Tomorrow if I have time, I will take photos of the family and the house **I'm staying in** and **send you them/send them to you**.

: Next Saturday Mrs White *will* take me to the large shopping centre in Churchill Square.

Error: the use of '**will**' when it is unsuitable in the context.

Correction: Next Saturday Mrs White **is taking** me to ...

Next Saturday Mrs White **is going to take** me to ...

Notes: The present continuous is used with a future time expression when something is already arranged before speaking.

The '**be going to + infinitive**' form is used for plans or intentions made before speaking. In the above context both are possible depending on aspect (how the speaker perceives the situation).

Errors twenty nine and thirty: She *said me* there are more than eighty shops. I *want buy* some English clothes.

Error: she **told me** or she **said to me**. We can only use an object pronoun directly after '**tell**' but never directly after '**say**'.